This book belongs to:

_____

ありがとう
Arigato
Japanese

© Copyright 2021-2025- All rights reserved.

You may not reproduce, duplicate or send the contents of this book without direct written permission from the author. You cannot hereby despite any circumstance blame the publisher or hold him or her to legal responsibility for any reparation, compensations, or monetary forfeiture owing to the information included herein, either in a direct or an indirect way.

Legal Notice: This book has copyright protection. You can use the book for personal purpose. You should not sell, use, alter, distribute, quote, take excerpts or paraphrase in part or whole the material contained in this book without obtaining the permission of the author first.

Disclaimer Notice: You must take note that the information in this document is for casual reading and entertainment purposes only. We have made every attempt to provide accurate, up to date and reliable information. We do not express or imply guarantees of any kind. The persons who read admit that the writer is not occupied in giving legal, financial, medical or other advice. We put this book content by sourcing various places.

Please consult a licensed professional before you try any techniques shown in this book. By going through this document, the book lover comes to an agreement that under no situation is the author accountable for any forfeiture, direct or indirect, which they may incur because of the use of material contained in this document, including, but not limited to, —errors, omissions, or inaccuracies.

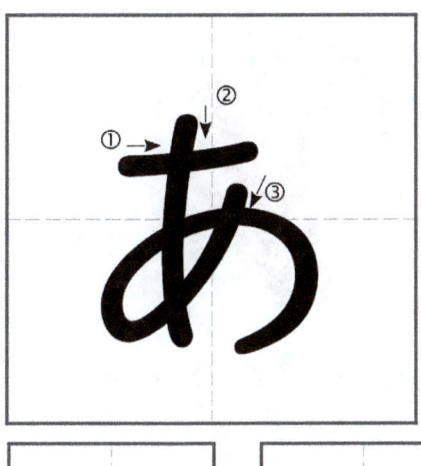

Rain: あめ 雨 *ame*

 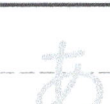

あ <a> is pronounced like in C<u>a</u>r.

あ い う え お

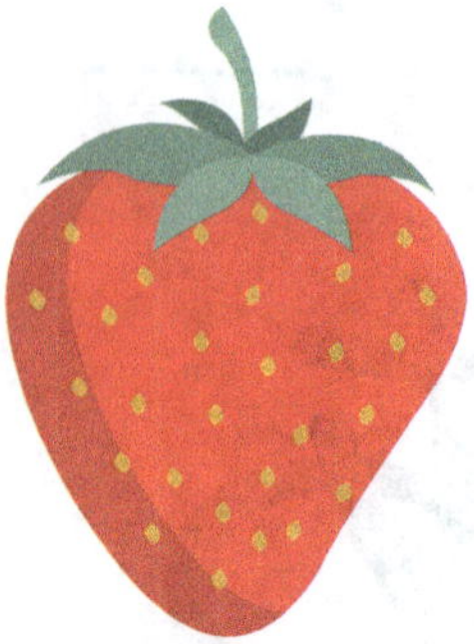

Strawberry: いちご 苺 *ichigo*

い <i> is pronounced like in **ee**l.

あ い う え お

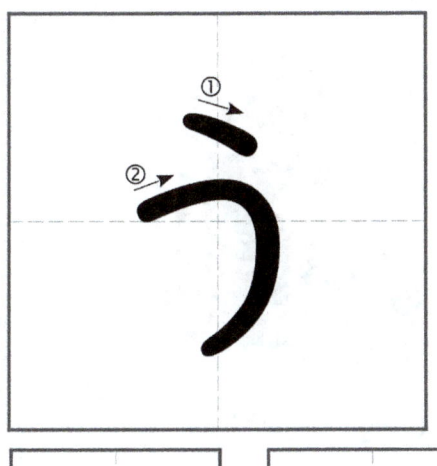

Ocean: うみ 海 umi

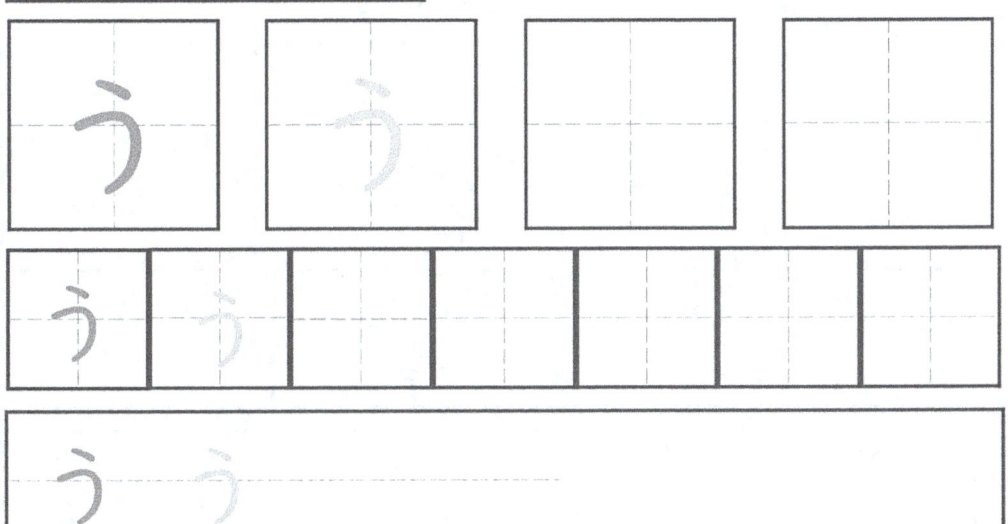

う <u> is pronounced like in **oo**ps!

あ い う え お

English (language): えいご 英語 *eigo*

え <e> is pronounced like in **e**gg.

あ い う **え** お

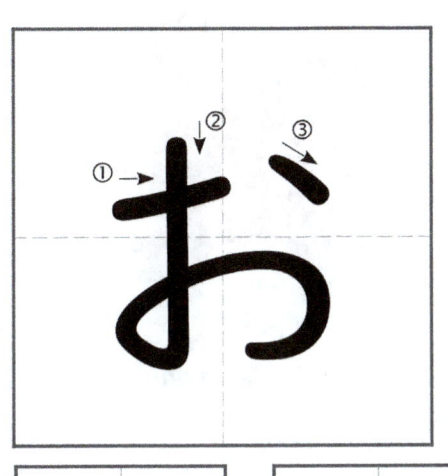
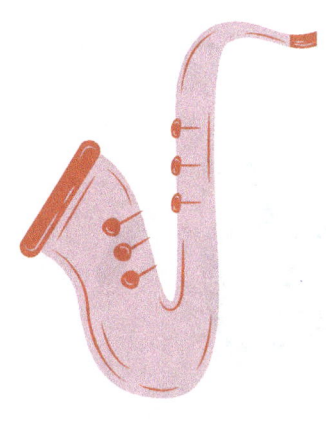

Music: おんがく 音楽 *ongagku*

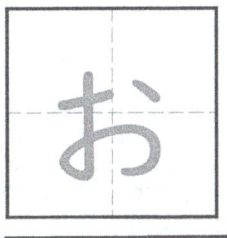 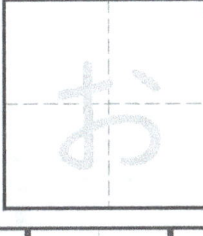  

お <o> is pronounced like in <u>oh</u>.

あ い う え お

Crab: かに 蟹 *kani*

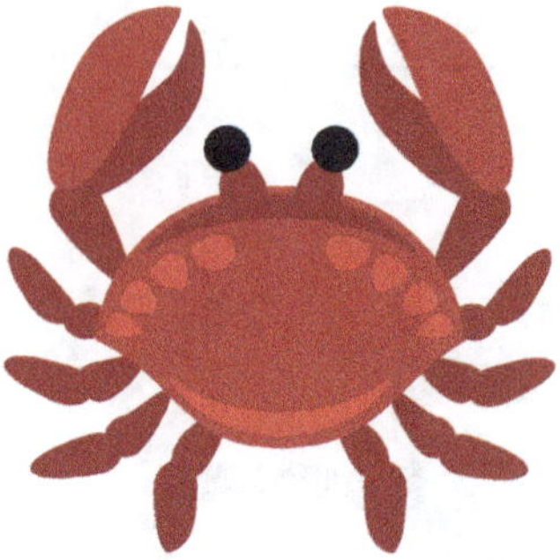

か <ka> is just the "K" sounds plus あ.

か き く け こ

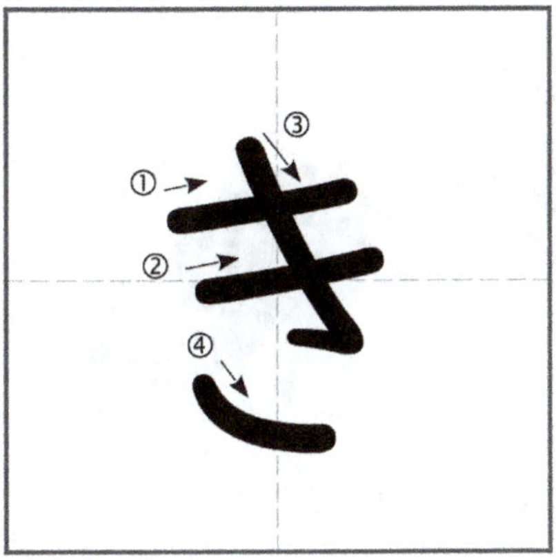

Giraffe: きりん　麒麟　*kirin*

き <ki> is just the "K" sounds plus い.

ありがとう
Arigato
Japanese

か　き　く　け　こ

Shoes: くつ 靴 *kutsu*

く <ku> is just the "K" sounds plus う.

ありがとう
Arigato
Japanese

か き く け こ

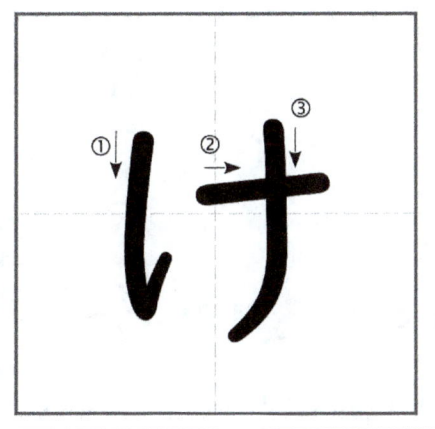

Police: けいさつ 警察 *keisatsu*

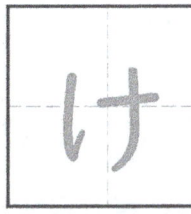   

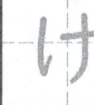 

け <ke> is just the "K" sounds plus え.

か　き　く　**け**　こ

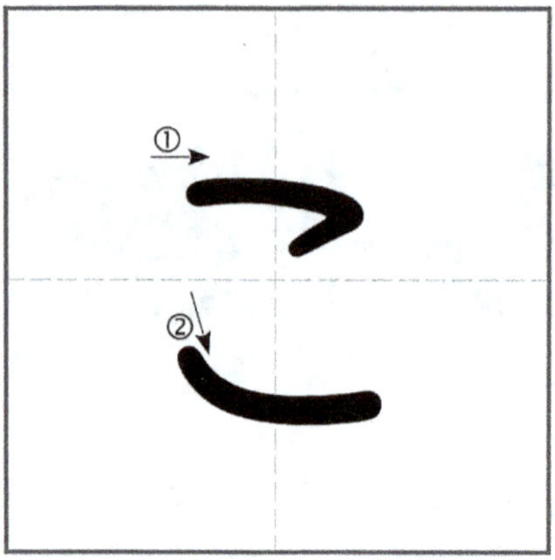

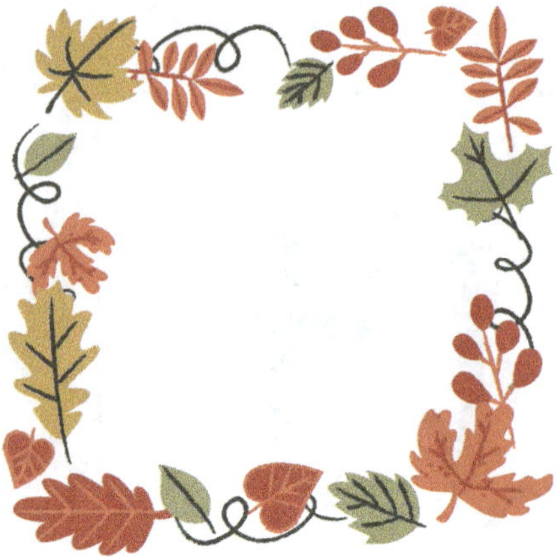

こ

Autumn foliage: こうよう 紅葉 *kouyou*

こ <ko> is just the "K" sounds plus お.

か き く け こ

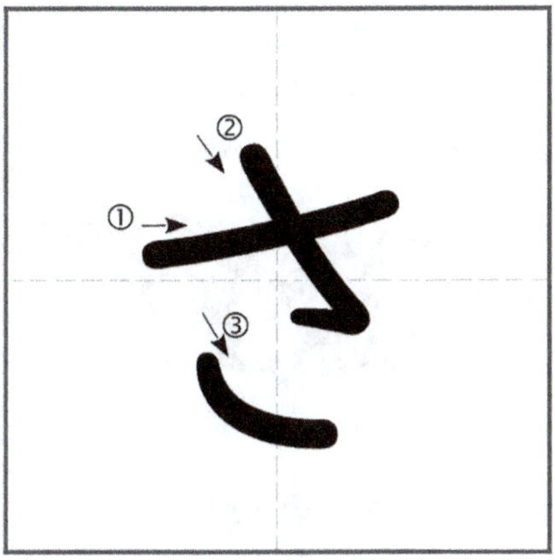

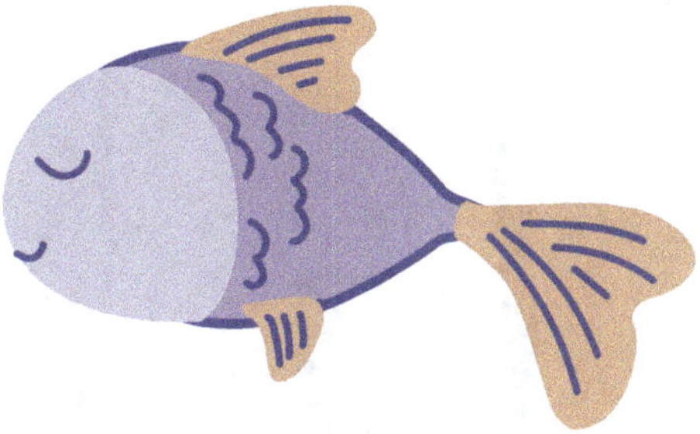

Fish: さかな　魚　*sakana*

さ さ

さ さ

さ さ

さ <sa> is just the “S” sounds plus あ .

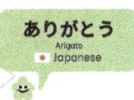

さ　し　す　せ　そ

Salt: しお 塩 *shio*

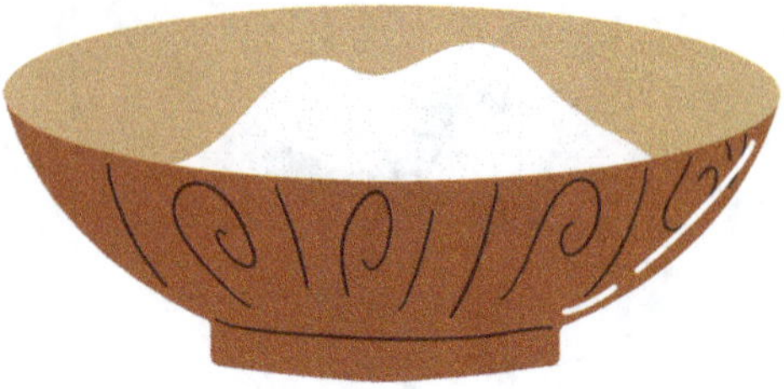

し \<Shi\> is just the "Sh" sounds plus い.
exception: Instead of "si", it is "shi."

さ し す せ そ

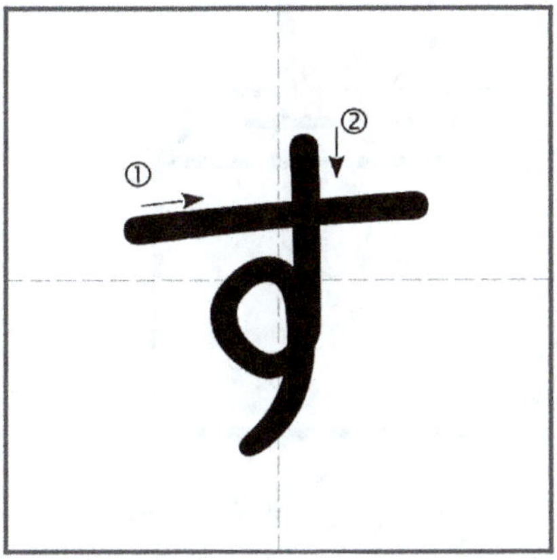

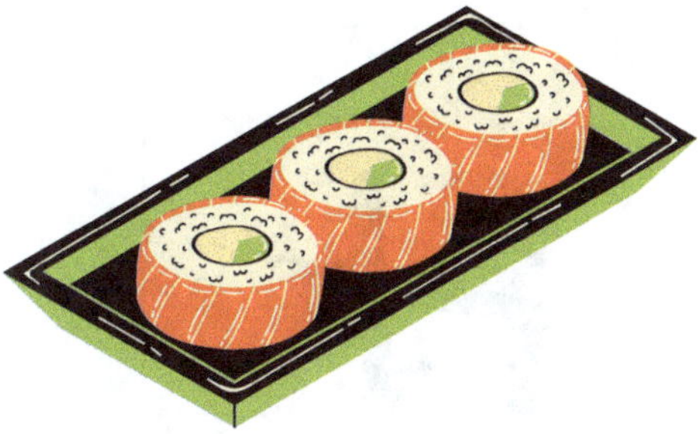

Sushi: すし 寿司 *Sushi*

す <su> is just the "S" sounds plus う.

さ し す せ そ

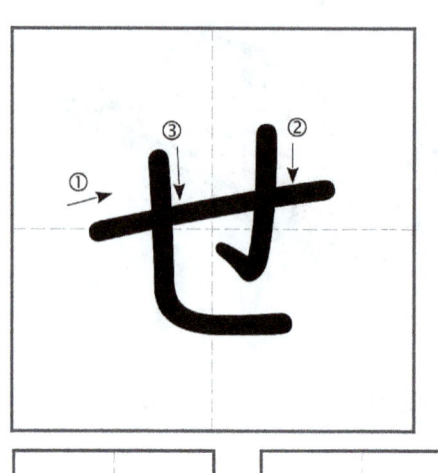

Election: せんきょ 選挙 *senkyo*

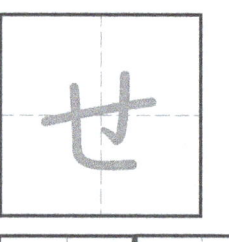 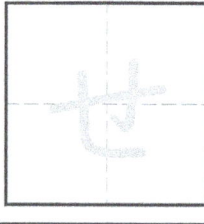  

せ <se> is just the "S" sounds plus え．

さ　し　す　**せ**　そ

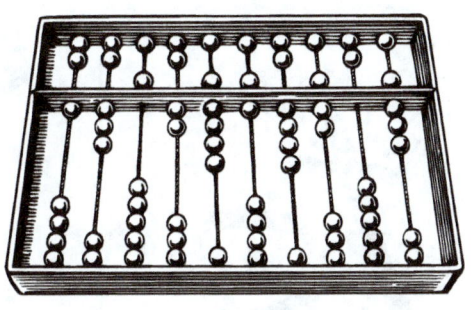

Abacus: そろばん　算盤　*soroban*

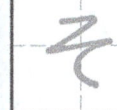 

そ <so> is just the "S" sounds plus お．

さ　し　す　せ　そ

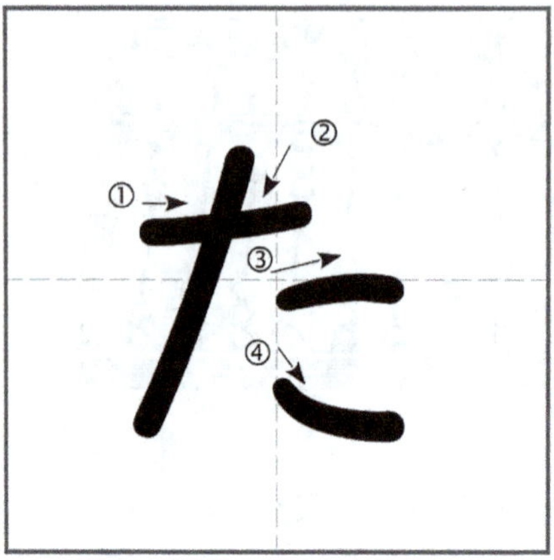

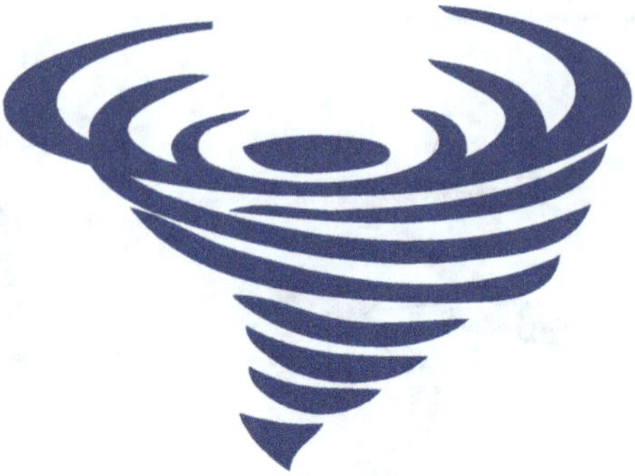

Typhoon: たいふう　台風　*taihuu*

た <ta> is just the "T" sounds plus あ.

た　ち　つ　て　と

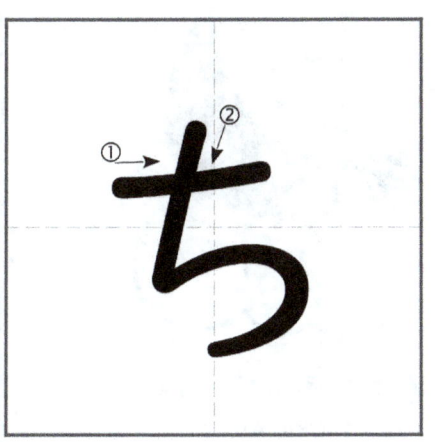

Subway: ちかてつ 地下鉄 *chikatetsu*

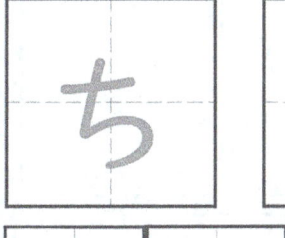 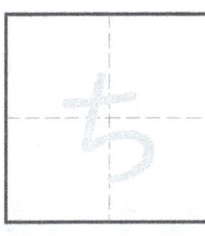  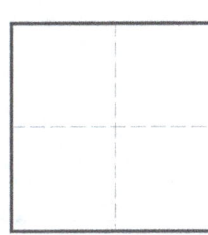

ち <Chi> is just the "Ch" sounds plus い.
exception: Instead of "ti", it is "chi."

た　ち　っ　て　と

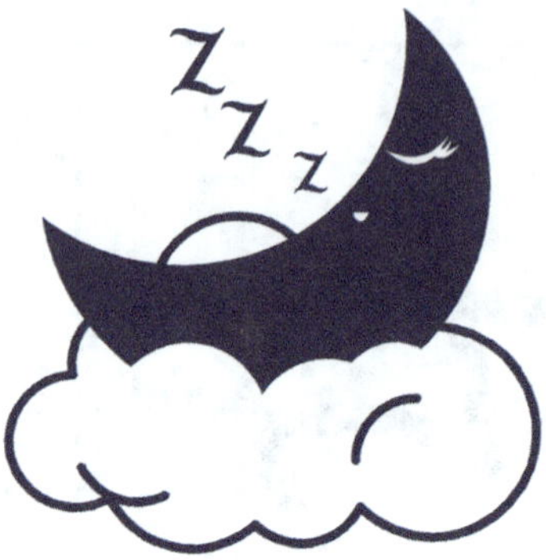

Moonlight: つきあかり　月明かり
tsukiakari

つ <tsu> is just the "Ts" sounds plus う.

たちつてと

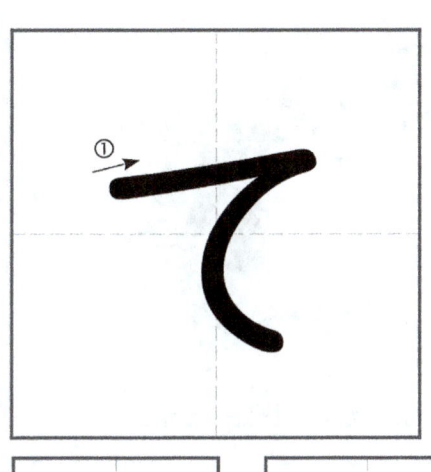

Temple: てら 寺 tera

て <te> is just the "T" sounds plus え.

た ち っ て と

Lizard: とかげ 蜥蜴 *tokage*

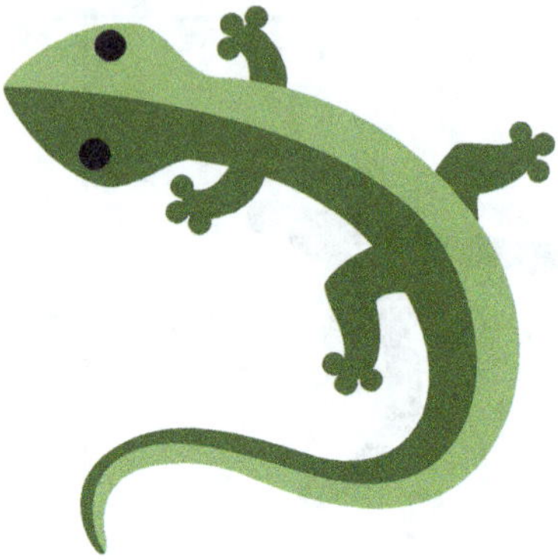

と <to> is just the "T" sounds plus お.

ありがとう
Arigato
Japanese

た ち つ て と

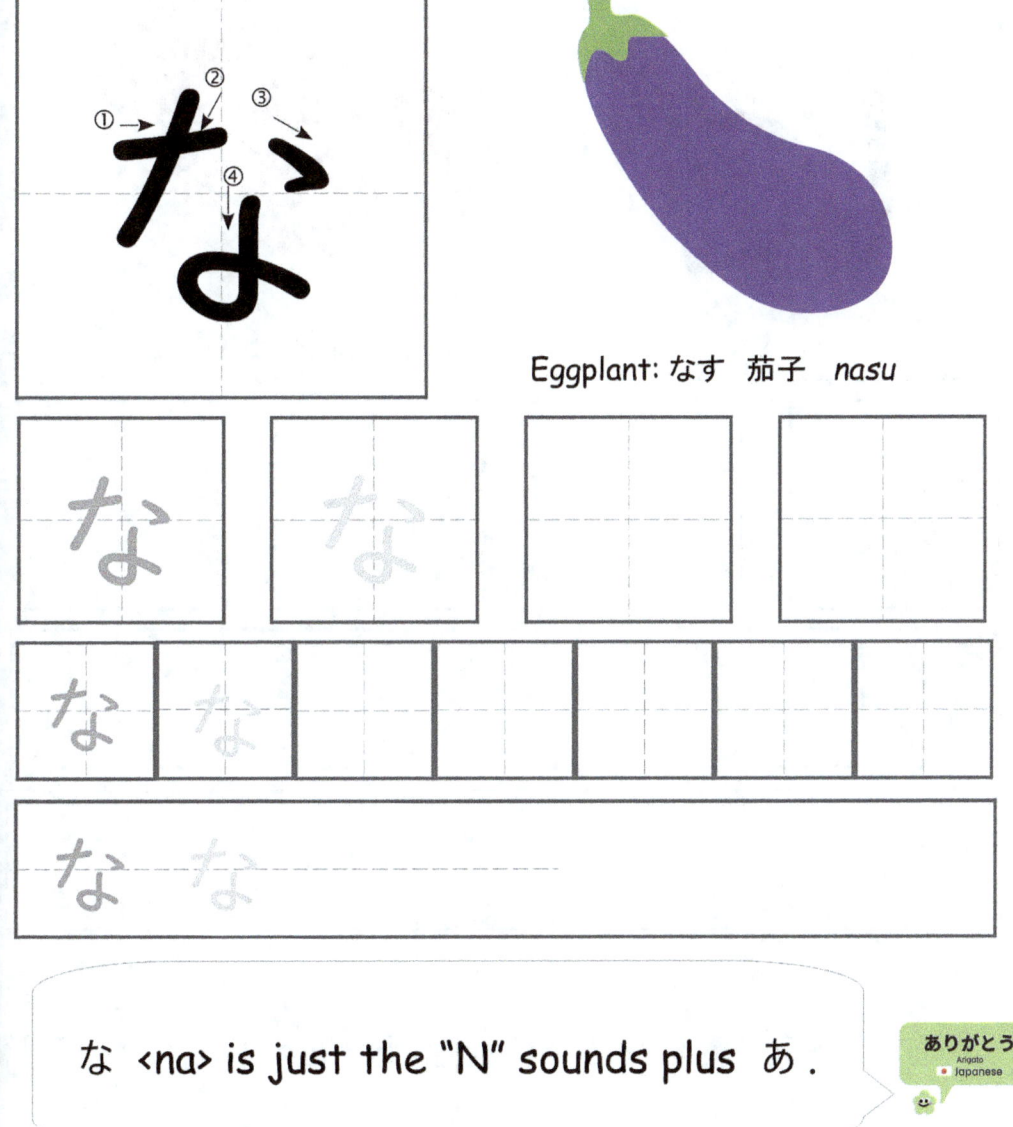

Eggplant: なす 茄子 *nasu*

な <na> is just the "N" sounds plus あ.

ありがとう
Arigato
Japanese

な に ぬ ね の

Meat: にく 肉 *niku*

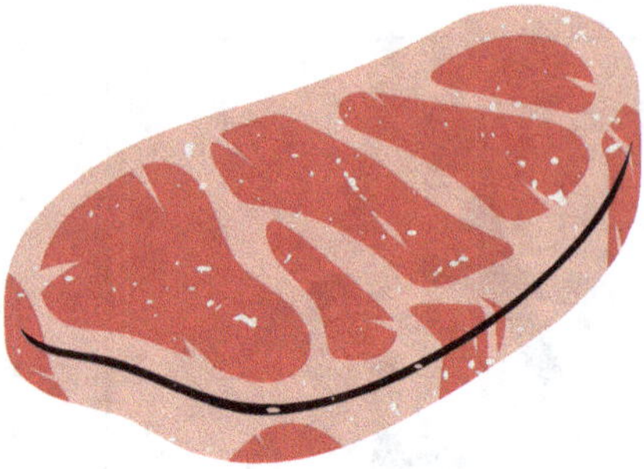

に \<ni\> is just the "N" sounds plus い.

ありがとう
Arigato
Japanese

な に ぬ ね の

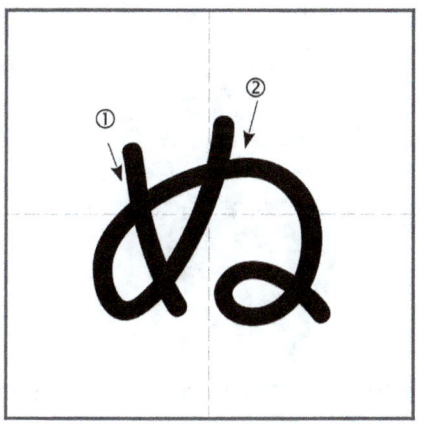

Coloring: ぬりえ　塗り絵　*nurie*

 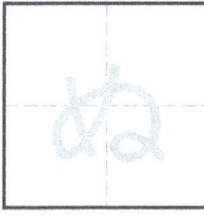  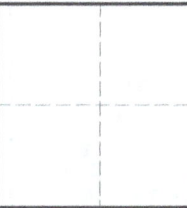

 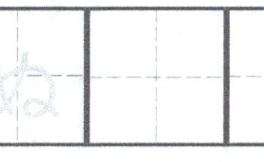 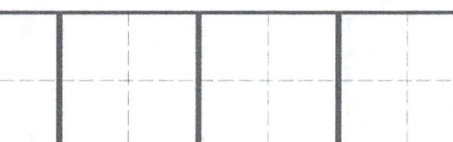

ぬ <nu> is just the "N" sounds plus う.

ありがとう
Arigato
Japanese

な　に　**ぬ**　ね　の

Tax Payment: のうぜい　納税　*nouzei*

の \<no\> is just the "N" sounds plus お.

な　に　ぬ　ね　の

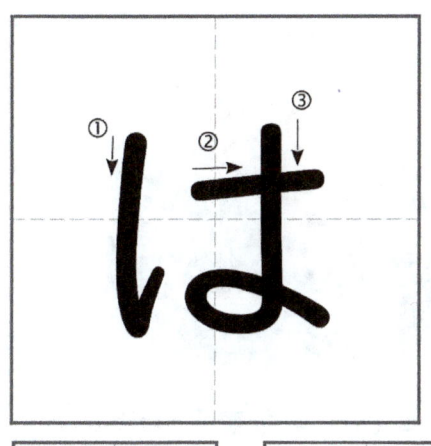

Honey: はちみつ 蜂蜜 *hachimitsu*

は <ha> is just the "H" sounds plus あ.

は ひ ふ へ ほ

ひ

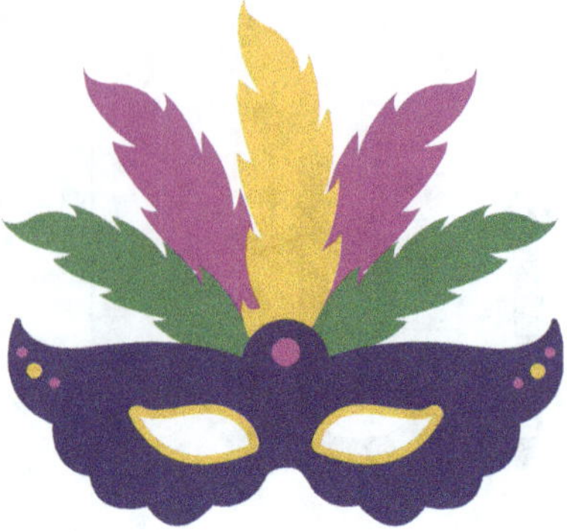

Secret: ひみつ　秘密　*himitsu*

ひ ひ

ひ ひ

ひ ひ

ひ <hi> is just the "H" sounds plus い.

は　ひ　ふ　へ　ほ

Railroad Crossing: ふみきり 踏切
fumikiri

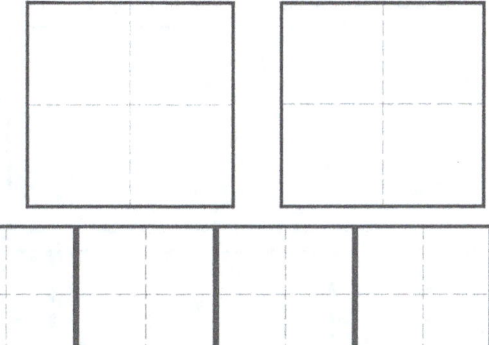

ふ <fu/hu> is just the "F/H" sounds plus う.

は ひ **ふ** へ ほ

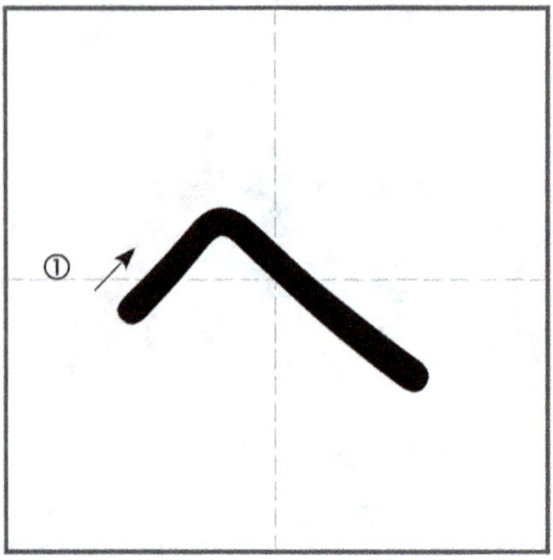

Weekdays: へいじつ 平日 *heijitsu*

へ <he> is just the "H" sounds plus え.

は　ひ　ふ　へ　ほ

Star: ほし 星 *hoshi*

ほ <ho> is just the "H" sounds plus お.

は　ひ　ふ　へ　**ほ**

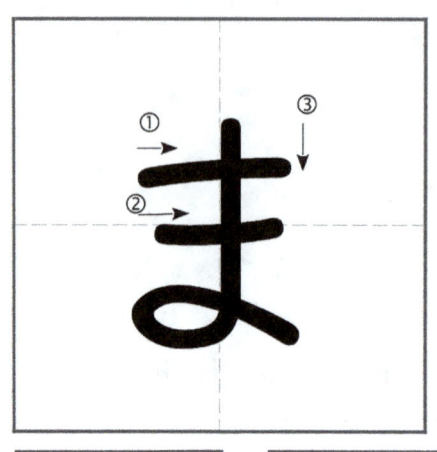

Comics: まんが 漢画 *manga*

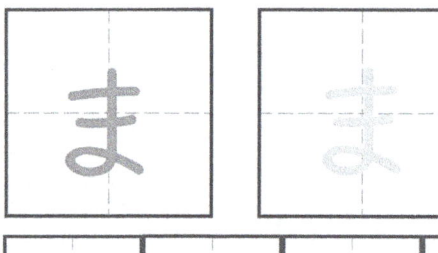
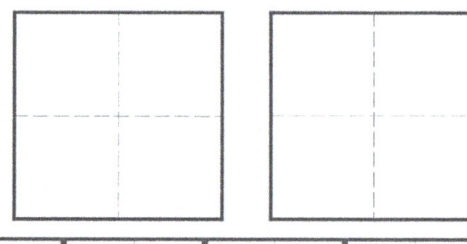
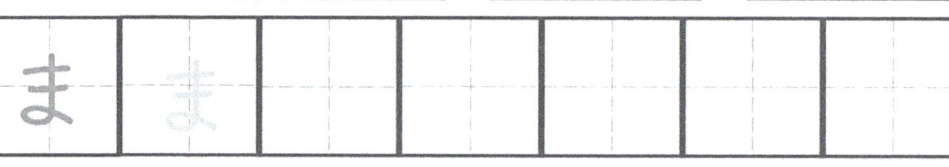

ま <ma> is just the "M" sounds plus あ.

まみむめも

Harbor/Port: みなと 港 *minato*

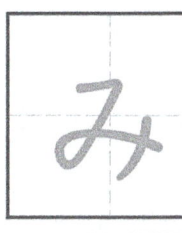 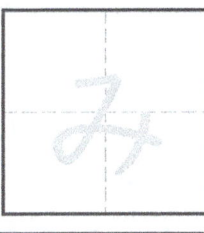

み <mi> is just the "M" sounds plus い.

ま **み** む め も

Insect: むし 虫 *mushi*

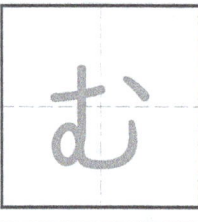   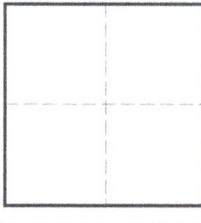

む \<mu\> is just the "M" sounds plus う.

ま み **む** め も

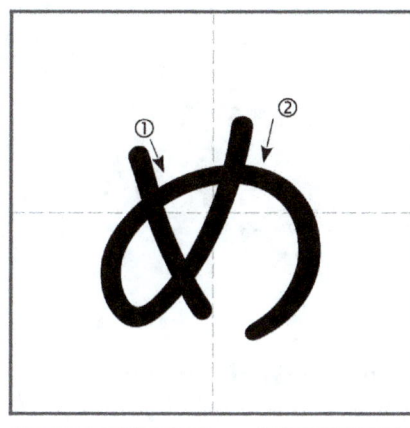

Glasses: めがね 眼鏡 *megane*

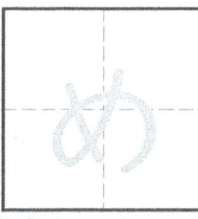

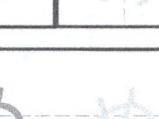

め \<me\> is just the "M" sounds plus え.

Rice cake: もち 餅 *mochi*

も <mo> is just the "M" sounds plus お.

ま み む め **も**

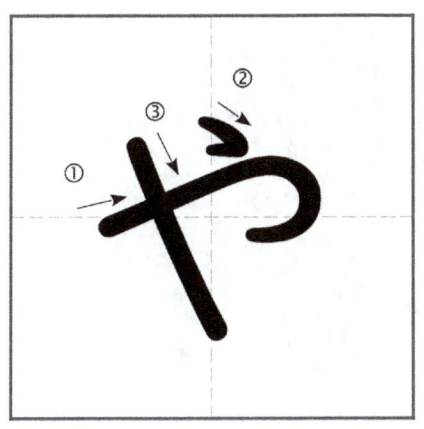

Vegetables: やさい 野菜 *yasai*

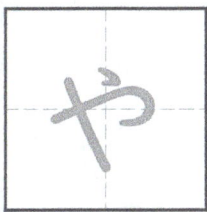  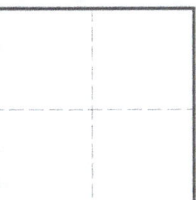 

や \<ya\> is just the "Y" sounds plus あ.

や （） ゆ （） よ

①ゑ

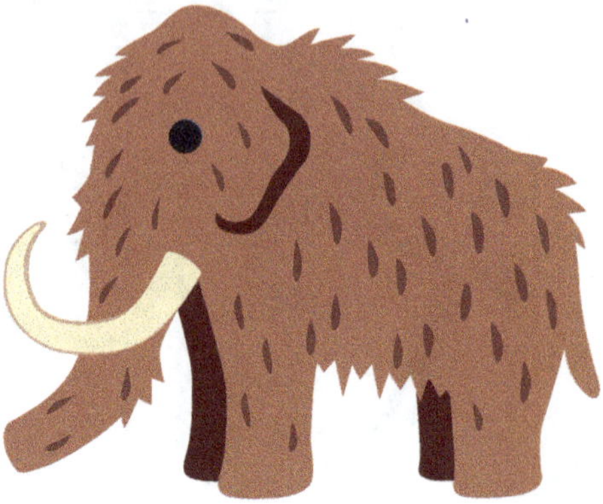

ゑ ゑ

ゑ ゑ

ゑ ゑ

ゑ was deemed obsolete in Japan, and replaced with え in 1946. It is now rare in everyday usage and you may find it in proper nouns.

ありがとう
Arigato
Japanese

や (ゐ) ゆ (ゑ) よ

Snow: ゆき 雪 *yuki*

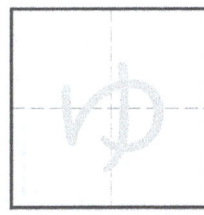

ゆ <yu> is just the "Y" sounds plus う.

ゑ was deemed obsolete in Japan, and replaced with え in 1946. It is now rare in everyday usage and you may find it in proper nouns.

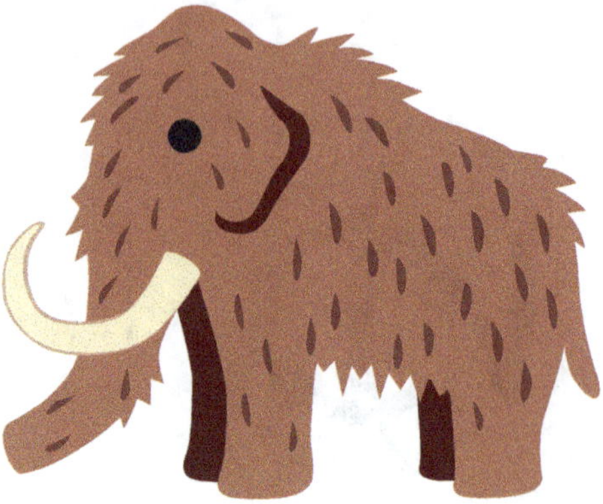

や (ゐ) ゆ (**ゑ**) よ

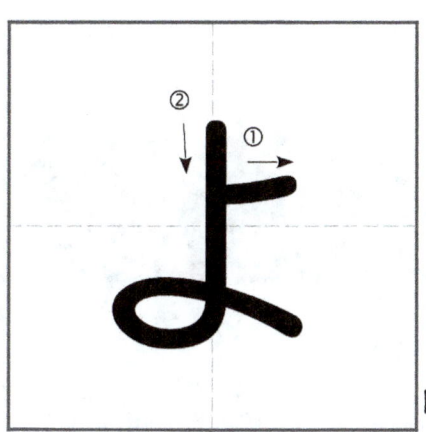

Night owl: よふかし 夜更かし　*yofukashi*

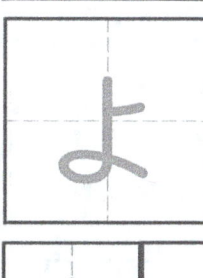   

よ <yo> is just the "Y" sounds plus お.

ありがとう
Arigato
Japanese

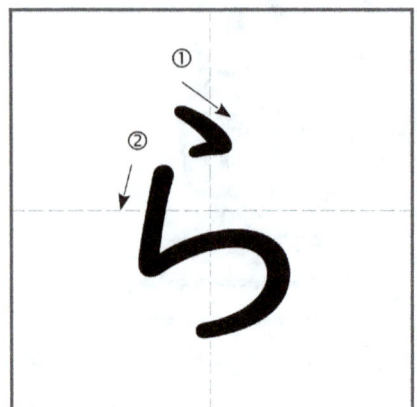

Graffiti: らくがき 落書き　rakugaki

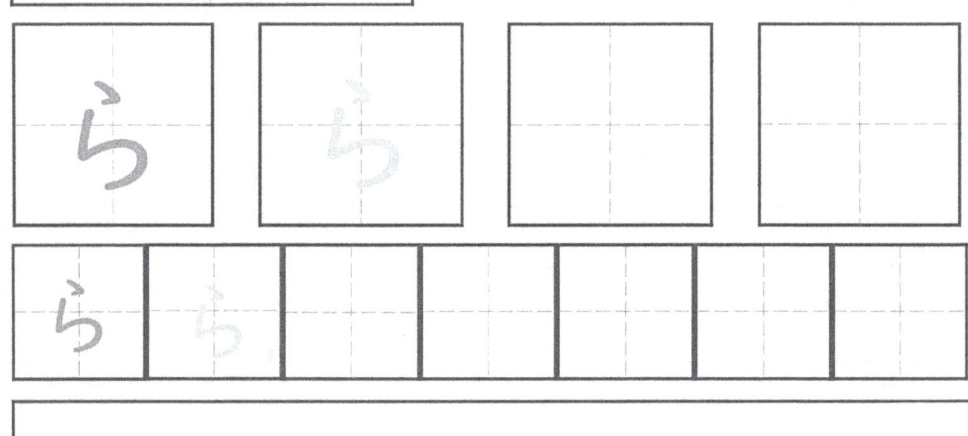

ら <ra> is just the "R" sounds plus あ.
R-Column pronunciation may be difficult to native English speakers. It sounds like between "R" and "L".

ありがとう
Arigato
Japanese

| ら | り | る | れ | ろ |

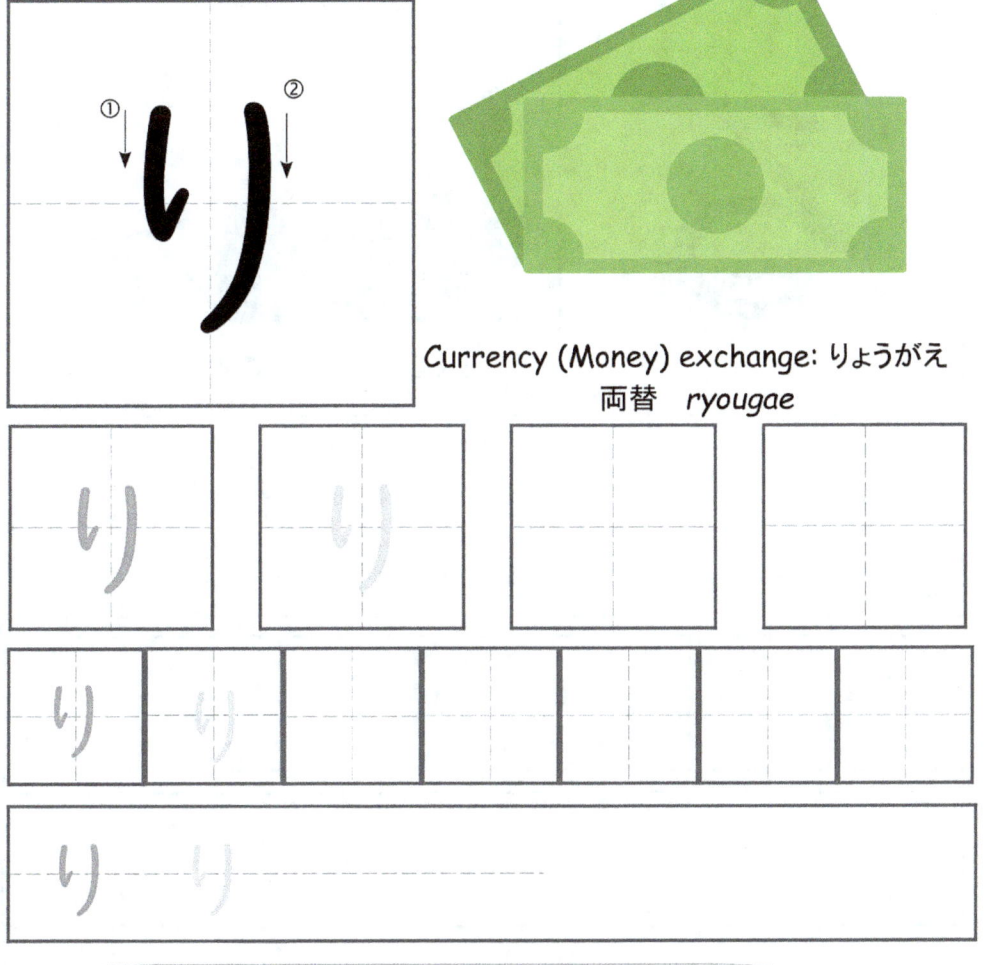

Currency (Money) exchange: りょうがえ
両替　*ryougae*

り <ri> is just the "R" sounds plus い.
R-Column pronunciation may be difficult to native English speakers. It sounds like between "R" and "L".

ありがとう
Arigato
Japanese

ら　り　る　れ　ろ

Azure: るりいろ 瑠璃色 *ruriiro*

  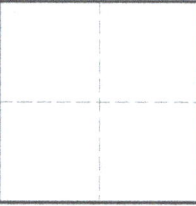 

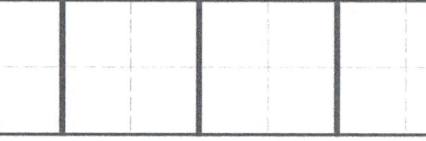

> る <ru> is just the "R" sounds plus う.
> *R-Column pronunciation may be difficult to native English speakers. It sounds like between "R" and "L".*

ありがとう
Arigato
japanese

ら り **る** れ ろ

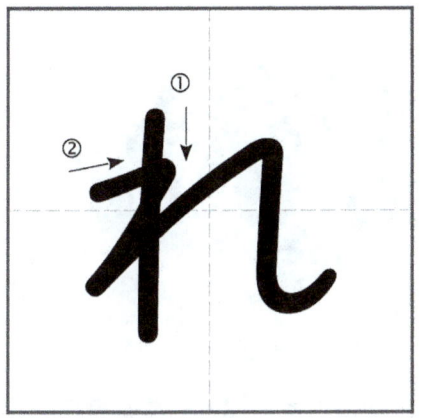

THANKYOU

Courtesy: れいぎ 礼儀 *reigi*

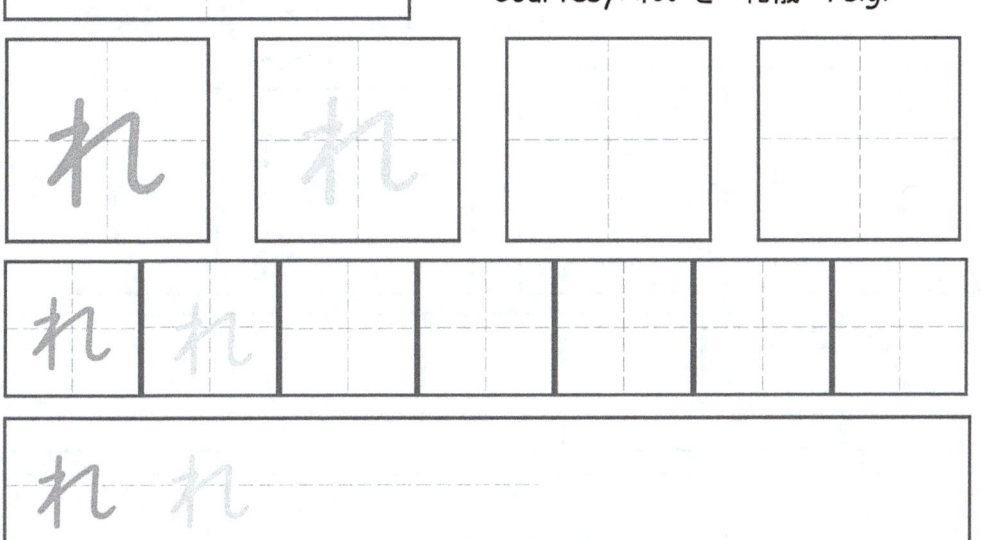

れ <re> is just the "R" sounds plus え.
R-Column pronunciation may be difficult to native English speakers. It sounds like between "R" and "L".

ろ

Open-air bath: ろてんぶろ　露天風呂
rotenburo

ろ \<ro\> is just the "R" sounds plus お.
R-Column pronunciation may be difficult to native English speakers. It sounds like between "R" and "L".

ら　り　る　れ　ろ

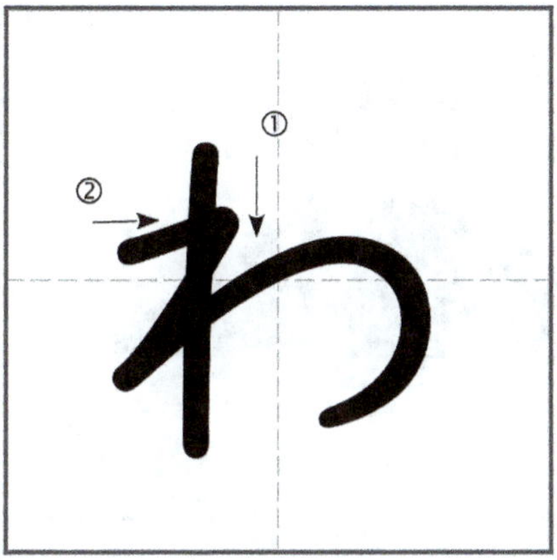

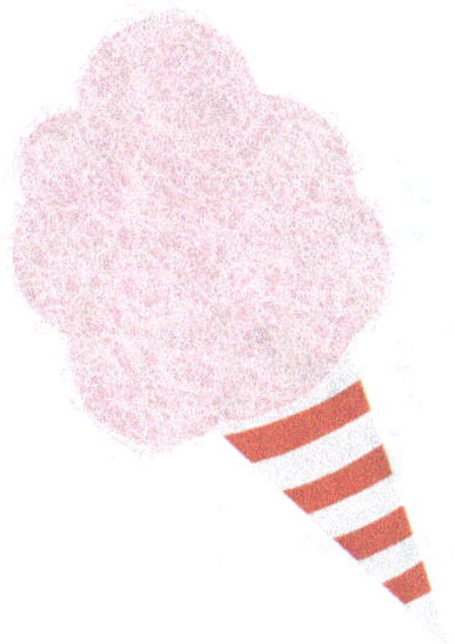

Cotton candy: わたあめ　綿飴　*wataame*

わ <wa> is just the "W" sounds plus あ .

わ を ん

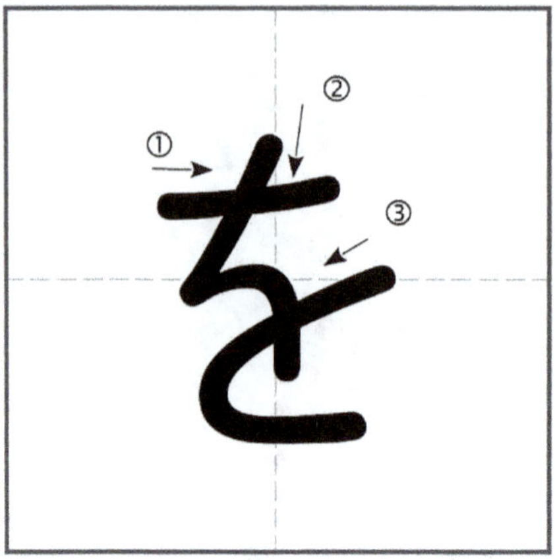

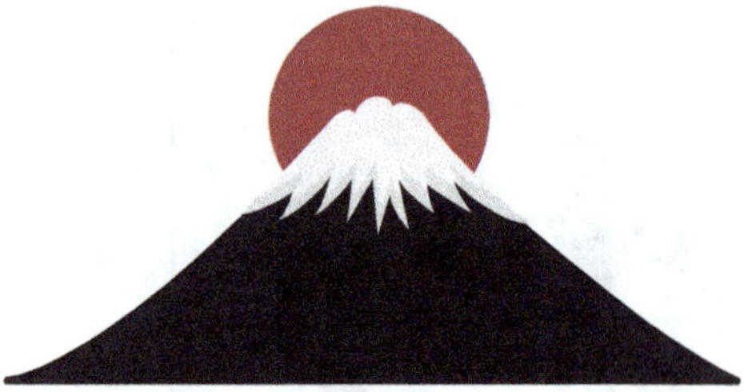

を <wo> is just the "W" sounds plus お,
but you don't need to pronounce "W" too much!
In 1946, all of the を were replaced to お excepting
grammatical terms relating to the particle.

わ　を　ん

ん

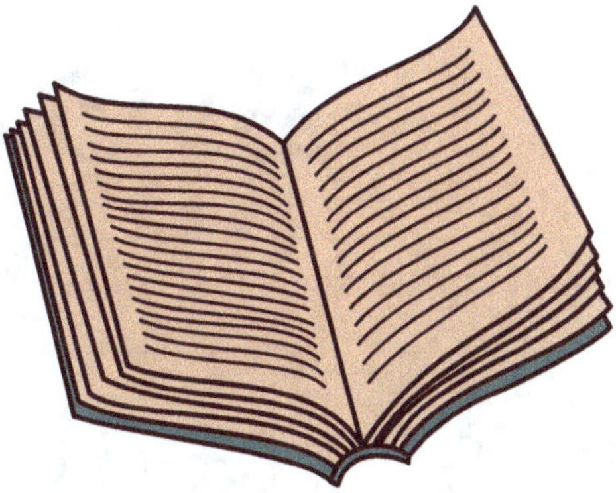

Book: ほん 本 *hon*

ん is just the "n" sound.
There is no words starting from ん.

わ を ん

あいうえお表

W	R	Y	M	H	N	T	S	K	Column / Vowel
わ	ら	や	ま	は	な	た	さ	か	あ a
	り	ゐ	み	ひ	に	ち (chi)	し (shi)	き	い i
	る	ゆ	む	ふ	ぬ	つ (tsu)	す	く	う u
	れ	ゑ	め	へ	ね	て	せ	け	え e
を	ろ	よ	も	ほ	の	と	そ	こ	お o
ん n									

ありがとう

Arigato

 Japanese